Summary and Analysis of

MAN'S SEARCH FOR MEANING

Based on the Book by Viktor E. Frankl

WORTH BOOKS
SMART SUMMARIES

This Worth Books book is based on the 1984 paperback edition of *Man's Search for Meaning* by Viktor E. Frankl, published by Simon & Schuster.

Summary and analysis copyright © 2017 by Open Road Integrated Media, Inc.

ISBN: 978-1-5040-4677-0

Worth Books
180 Maiden Lane
Suite 8A
New York, NY 10038
www.worthbooks.com

WORTH BOOKS
SMART SUMMARIES

Worth Books is a division of Open Road Integrated Media, Inc.

Contents

Context

During World War II (1939–1945), millions of people suffered the physical and existential terror of the Nazi concentration camps. The names now are famous: Dachau, Buchenwald, Auschwitz-Birkenau (the largest—and, unlike the others, a combined death camp and labor camp). At the time war was declared, Viktor E. Frankl was a respected psychiatrist at the Rothschild Hospital in Vienna, Austria. His work had already made a great impact in his field. He had begun several highly successful programs to treat suicidal patients, and his opinions on psychological matters were highly sought-after across Europe, even by well-respected psychoanalysts such as Wilhelm Reich and Sigmund Freud. After the Nazi *Anschluss*—the

German occupation of Austria—in 1938, Frankl was legally disallowed from treating Aryans, or non-Jews. Along with millions of other Jews, he and his family were persecuted and eventually detained in Theresienstadt and Auschwitz. A successful psychiatrist with a probing mind, Frankl used much of what he'd learned about human psychology to survive—and help others survive—the camps. After a long and brutal imprisonment, during which almost all of his family perished, he was one of the few to walk out of Auschwitz at the end of the war.

Frankl wrote a book about his experiences, describing in detail the lessons in human psychology he had gleaned from the extreme conditions of the camps. *Nevertheless, Say "Yes" to Life*, written in German and distributed under many other titles, was published anonymously in 1946, since Frankl didn't believe it would have much public impact. But demand for the book soon grew. When the English translation, titled *Man's Search for Meaning*, was finally published in 1959, it sold millions of copies. To this day, it is reprinted regularly.

The central idea of Frankl's work was the practice of "logotherapy," a Greek-based term that more or less translates to "meaning therapy." Never as broadly popularized as Freud's psychotherapy or Rogerian group therapy, logotherapy is nonetheless spectacularly effective in treating patients with suicidal thoughts, midlife crises, depression, and various other conditions. The process of logotherapy involves seeking out, discovering, and naming what can be said to be the true meaning of your individual life, whether that meaning centers on love, family, work, or something else.

Since his death in 1997, Frankl's work has been carried forward in numerous logotherapy institutes across the world. His most popular book, *Man's Search for Meaning*, remains a classic that continues to be read by new generations each decade.

Overview

Viktor Frankl's classic *Man's Search for Meaning* can be seen as both a memoir of his years in Nazi concentration camps and a founding document for the field of logotherapy. The first and largest section of the book covers Frankl's own experiences in both large and small camps across Nazi-occupied territory, going into vivid detail about the conditions, agonies, and day-to-day grind of being a prisoner under a criminal regime in Europe. He makes the point, though, that the story he tells is not about the "heroes and martyrs" fighting tyranny *in extremis*, but rather the common experiences of regular prisoners—average family people and workers—many of whom he watched die in the camps.

The experience of a Nazi concentration camp is one of unimaginable suffering. The all-powerful institution of violence and coercion effectively controlled every aspect of daily life for Frankl and the other prisoners, leaving little room for the ordinary. The camps were a reality unto themselves—allowing no communication with the outside world—and the daily experience of violence, murder, starvation, and deprivation kept the surviving inmates disempowered and docile. Still, Frankl discovered some surprising things about human resilience and psychology, ideas that challenged the era's preconceptions about physical and mental well-being. How was it that people could survive such an ordeal? What kinds of reactions did different people have, and could those reactions be examined and categorized?

Frankl was already a well-known doctor at the Rothschild Hospital in Vienna, and inmates and Nazi officials alike sought after his expertise during his time in the camps. His background and profession proved useful. He was stationed in the "typhus block," where he aided the sick—though it wasn't much of a recovery clinic—and occasionally one of the guards took a liking to him for his willingness to listen to personal stories and offer advice. Because of this, Frankl had more consistent and regular interaction with the variety of personalities there, and he was able to see things both from the perspective of

the officials and from the viewpoint of enslaved labor-
ers—the thriving and the dying.

In secret, he took shorthand notes on scraps
of paper, remarking on the notable or widespread
responses of moral apathy, depersonalization, extin-
guished sex drive, gallows humor, suicidal tendencies,
and the physical and emotional responses of people
when subjected to long-term starvation and sleep
deprivation. Frankl noted that suffering, whether
a small or large amount of it, "completely fills the
human soul and conscious mind," making ordinary
existence impossible and stoking a range of reactions
that would be impossible to imagine in any other circumstances.

Still, the book offers insights on and a direct challenge to the idea of "surviving" that is still the accepted
notion today, providing a reasoned contradiction of
the idea that only the strong make it through while
the weak perish. In many ways, Frankl found the
opposite to be true. He describes young, healthy,
physically exemplary prisoners who were some of the
first to perish, noting to himself, with some surprise,
that someone who was physically weaker often had
a better chance of surviving if he had a "rich inner
life." This was where Frankl began to take note of
the power of meaningfulness in a person's life. Intellectual life in the camp was totally absent, and those
prisoners who turned to their own memories of great

literature and ideas—Frankl quotes Dostoevsky, Tol-stoy, the Bible, Thomas Mann, and others—tended to have the moral stamina not only to survive, but also to act selflessly for others in the face of great personal risk. This idea became the basis for logotherapy.

In each individual case, a prisoner's unique psy-chopathology influenced his or her battle with the terrorizing influences of the camps. Frankl shares anecdotes about various experiences—and how those experiences led either to death or survival. The suf-fering in the camps brought out each individual's basest traits, and it was inevitably these characteris-tics—personal beliefs, inner life, moral quality—that defined that person's experience of life under heavy oppression. Once liberated from the camps, these traits would also shape the person's ability to cope in a free world.

Frankl's brief autobiographical document of con-centration camp life is one of the most detailed and psychologically interesting on record. There are other accounts of life in the camps—dramatizations and memoirs—but Frankl's training in psychology allowed him to remove himself and describe the activ-ities and events of the camp as a visiting third-party observer might. Reading his account, you not only come to understand the terrors and unlivable condi-tions of the camps, but also begin to imagine yourself coping with the horrifying circumstances. What are your most basic personality and moral traits? What is at the core of meaningfulness in your own life? These and other questions will inevitably define your own search for meaning.

In the postscript and afterword, in light of his description of concentration camp life, Frankl tasks himself with explaining for the lay reader the nature and usefulness of his own school of psychotherapy: logotherapy. He also discusses his idea of "tragic optimism" in the face of life's "tragic triad": pain, guilt, and death. The psychiatric approach has many aspects to it—including noö-dynamics, noögenic neuroses, existential frustration—and Frankl largely makes use of anecdotal evidence to make his case for his theories.

It may go without saying that, after he was released from the camps, Frankl eventually returned to his work with a fresh enthusiasm and armed with the unique insights he gained by experiencing one of history's most horrific events of systemic oppression. He died in 1997, a celebrated proponent of the meaningful life.

Summary

I. Experiences in a Concentration Camp

Frankl begins with the institutional brutality of his own entry into the camps: the formal orderliness with which Nazi officials organized transport, admission, regulation, and control of the prisoners. The processing of prisoners—giving them numbers, dividing them up into random groups, stripping them naked, beating them, selecting privileged capos, setting them to work from early in the morning to late in the day, and starving them—in Frankl's estimation was a way of depriving people of their connections to others and to their own lives and histories. As a manner of control, this was very effective. People were too frightened, alienated, and intent on surviving to even consider resistance. The Nazis projected an image of total control and order, and an essential part of this was weakening and disempowering their prisoners.

Thoughts of suicide, fear of death, and brutal working conditions kept the prisoners down, but Frankl recounts moments where human behavior seemed to run counter to what was—and often still is—popularly thought about human psychology. Some obedient prisoners were selected by the Nazis and became capos—helpers and orderlies of the regime—but more often, prisoners would help strangers in the camp at great risk to themselves.

On his second day at Auschwitz, Frankl was approached by a man who broke the rules, risking death, by sneaking out to his hut to offer advice on how to survive in the camp. This deed was entirely selfless and also completely unnecessary, as it did little to help either party in the end.

Though suicide was possible—all one had to do was "run into the wire," the highly electrified fence surrounding the camp—few people actually killed themselves. And though many of those who repressed thoughts of suicide were still murdered, a small minority of survivors continued to take great risks for others and to find ways of maintaining calm, levelheadedness, and some optimism. Frankl found these cases the most interesting.

To understand better, Frankl broke the experience up into a few loose phases. The first phase was one of an ironic curiosity. Most inmates, subject to such hopelessness, moved into a state of removed curiosity as to how much pain they could take and whether they would survive. With the elimination of personal agency, it seemed that, initially, the intellectual mind took over and found itself stimulated to see what would happen next. How long could a person go without sleep? How long could a person stand out in two-degree weather without boots or a coat?

The brief first phase was then followed by a phase of apathy and a permanent and total lack of libido. Frankl viewed these characteristics as central symptoms of imprisonment. Prisoners began to view death and suffering as just another part of the day, unremarkable for the camps. Frankl too fell into this behavior, often viewing the body of a friend who died right in front of him or watching people ransack a dead body for a coat, shoes, and other possessions without the slightest reaction. He also had very few sexual thoughts and was reduced, essentially, to a state of physical and libidinal anhedonia or disinterest. These responses were characteristics of psychological self-defense and were necessary for survival. To feel, see, and live as normal in the camp was impossible, so in order to make it through the ordeal, the human mind naturally withdrew to a state of moral, physical, and emotional apathy.

Frankl discusses what he calls "cultural hibernation" and the importance of a rich inner life. The belief systems and culture of the prisoners were largely absent during internment, but Frankl writes that there were often heady discussions of a political, academic, or religious nature. This led him to some insights about the importance of intellectual lives for human beings. He remarks that the biggest and healthiest prisoners would often perish sooner than those with slighter constitutions who had rich intellectual lives. Inner peace and a desire to find meaning—through literature, science, theology, etc.—even when confronted with violence and chaos, was central not only to survival, but also to finding meaning in one's life. Frankl refers to his own knowledge of literature to aid his understanding of the range of human responses to the anguish. He quotes Lessing, "There are things which must cause you to lose your reason or you have none to lose," and Dostoevsky: "Yes, man can get used to anything, but do not ask how."

Thoughts of poetry, literature, and science helped Frankl to understand himself and the world around him and led to one of his central revelations. During a particularly difficult march in the cold, he recognized that he and other inmates were thinking of their wives in order to comfort themselves. Love was central, he thought, to survival and to finding meaning. "The salvation of man is through love and in love." The intensification of the inner life centering around thoughts of meaning and love gave the prisoners respite—if brief—from the moral and intellectual desolation of the camps.

Additional experiences, composing a kind of third phase of life in the camp, centered on the pursuit of "spiritual freedom." This struggle was the most intense and personal of all. It came out in various ways. Some people sang to one another or recited poems. In one case, a cabaret was put on for the group's entertainment. But psychological freedom was also found in brief or accidental respites: coming across a pair of old shoe laces, finding peas in your soup, doing something to help a friend.

Frankl did this last one often. He was once involved in a plan to break out from the camp and escape. He was excited, but also felt morally distraught over leaving his friends and patients behind. At the last minute, just when he and a friend were about to get away, he decided to remain behind to help his patients in the typhus block. Immediately, he felt better. Liberated, in a way. The struggle to maintain one's own values, he realized, was common among the prisoners. Many failed to find a way to do it. But others, like Frankl, did. Sacrificing oneself for others is, in the end, a way of surviving. It builds you up and makes you stronger, because it provides your life with meaning. Finally, Frankl quoted Dostoevsky to himself: "There is only one thing that I dread: not to be worthy of my sufferings."

Frankl brings this section of the book to a close with a long discussion of the choices we have in our own freedom. Psychological pressures, imprisonment, abuse, physical restraint—all of these have effects on the human mind. But for Frankl, it came down to the fact that we are able to choose to continue seeing value in living, and see ahead into the future and set goals, even in the most dire situations. The people who were able to do this not only survived, but also found peace and even happiness. Those who gave up perished.

Frankl tells a story of an inmate who had a dream predicting that the horrible war with Germany would be over on March 30, 1945. The man pinned all of his hopes on it. For the weeks and months leading up to that date, he was healthy and optimistic, completely believing in his dream. He'd given himself a goal, a small hope, and it opened up a world of optimism in him. But as March 30, 1945, drew closer and there was no sign of the war ending, the man fell ill. In the final days of March, he grew worse and worse until there was no hope. And on March 30, he died.

Frankl says that what people like this inmate knew

at first, but later forgot, was the idea that "it [does] not really matter what we [expect] from life, but rather what life [expects] from us." One cannot force his way in the world by pinning all his hopes on a single date on the calendar, because in the end, life teaches you how to live; it has its own expectations. The response to life—the choice a person must make to maintain hope and inner richness—will dictate whether and how well he or she survives. In some cases, it may be a person's individual fate to suffer. In this instance, it is the acceptance of this that brings liberation and meaning into that person's life. Those who are able to see this, whether consciously or not, find inner peace.

Need to Know: From 1942 to 1945, Austrian therapist Dr. Viktor Frankl was detained in various Nazi concentration camps throughout occupied Europe. Although existence for prisoners was dire agony beyond imagining, Frankl noted that those who survived tended to be individuals who found meaning and *inner richness* in their lives. An inner life that centered on love and selflessness, even at great personal risk, would eventually lead to a revelatory inner liberation. Phases of ironic curiosity, apathy, suicidal tendencies, and the suppression of spiritual freedom were experienced by all in the camp, but those who found meaning in the smallest consolations—memories, literature, song, generosity—were those who were able to "say yes" to life and maintain hope, and therefore find spiritual liberation. These experiences led Frankl not only to insights about psychological suffering and the human mind, but also about the very nature of life itself. According to his assessments, it will not do to have expectations of life. You only find freedom in realizing that life itself has expectations of you. Accepting this idea is critical to living a psychologically healthy life and finding meaning.

II. Logotherapy in a Nutshell

Logotherapy is a "meaning-based" therapy, a treatment based on what Frankl observes is man's universal search for meaning. He calls it "The Third Viennese School of Psychotherapy," next to Freudian psychology ("the will to pleasure") and Adlerian psychology ("the will to power"). Frankl's work is based on the idea of the "will to meaning." A lack of meaning is called *existential frustration* and typically results in a person being depressed because he or she feels there is no meaning in life. This existential state leads to "noögenic neuroses" (from *noös*, meaning mind), which typically presents itself as depression or dissatisfaction.

The neuroses emerge on the basis of "noö-dynamics," based on the idea of necessary tension between what one has achieved and what one ought to achieve. When there is no tension in life—that is, no goal or hope—one reaches a state of "homeostasis," or equilibrium, and this leads to depression. Although equilibrium is generally seen as the proper end state in other schools of therapy, Frankl sees it as dangerous. Without that tension, that motivation to do and produce in the world, depression, dissatisfaction, or even suicidal tendencies emerge. In other words, a person must have some use in the world, some reason for existing, that drives him forward.

Frankl then describes the *existential vacuum*, a historical concept. Frankl says that at some point in ancient history, man lost animal instincts that provided security, survival, a reason for living. Then, many thousands of years later, in our modern era, man lost "tradition," which may refer to religious, familial, or some other form of tradition that operates as a guide in one's life. With mass production, the centralization of power, and a general increase in life's comforts, people found themselves with less meaning or reason to go forward. Frankl notes that as many as 25% of the people in Europe were (at the time of writing) experiencing agony in this existential vacuum. In America, he interestingly notes, this figure rose to 60%.

As a way of treating this, each patient must search for his own *meaning of life* and *essence of existence*. This differs from patient to patient; there is no universal answer. Frankl writes that one must confront life's finiteness, as well as its finality, and freely choose to live as if he is being given a second chance to live *better*. Living meaningfully means responding to life's ever changing meaning. What life demands of a person may change from day to day, year to year. There are three basic ways to discover this changing meaning: by creating or doing some deed; by experiencing something or encountering someone; and by changing your attitude toward suffering.

It is through the *meaning of love* and the *meaning of suffering* that we are able to take hold of the core that makes up our personality and become free. Love helps us see our potential and suffering helps us see the final meaning. Although suffering is not necessary to find meaning, Frankl insists that in the right kind of life, it is possible to find meaning despite suffering. This meaning is discovered through examination and choice, and also through giving oneself over to life and its demands.

Through the "logodrama"—an instance in which our loss of or search for meaning is dramatized poignantly in our day-to-day life—we may discover what Frankl calls the "super-meaning." This super-meaning is the mystery of the cosmos, the fact that, despite all of our advancements and sciences and knowledge, there is still an indifferent universe out there about which we can never know anything. In such a context, our finiteness is clear, and it is through the acceptance of this that we may come to understand that the universe is not meaningless but rather has "unconditional meaningfulness."

As a small example of a logotherapy technique, Frankl offers the notions of "hyper-intention" and "hyper-reflection." Hyper-intention is the fear of something (such as failure) that finally brings about that which is feared. Frankl uses the example of a man who is afraid of blushing when he enters a room. Hyper-intention will cause that to happen. The opposite is also true—a forced intention will not bring about the desired outcome. Frankl's example is of a man wishing to prove his sexual potency. The more he tries to, the more he fails.

Hyper-reflection—the tendency to overthink and constantly imagine how one might fail—will bring about paralysis. Frankl's solution is to engage in "paradoxical intention." That is, the intentional embrace of the fear. If you fear sweating in public, as one of his patients did, the idea is to intentionally try to demonstrate how much you can sweat in public. Patients who underwent paradoxical intention found themselves losing their fears and finally being cured of them. Such a method can be applied to issues of sleep disturbance, public speaking, and many others.

There is also something Frankl calls *collective neuroses*, which is the current neurosis of any particular era. At the time of writing, he determined that nihilism was the most widespread problem. People felt then, and still do now, that life is nothing but a system of laws and organs and predetermined functions. This led to a mass sense of meaninglessness. As a result of this, and to some extent as a result of the influence of Freud, mankind fell into what he calls "pan-determinism," or the sense that we are determined by our childhoods and cannot really take a stand against adverse conditions (the way Frankl did during the Holocaust). But people, Frankl insists, are free to choose. It is this faculty in us that makes us more than merely our bodies, past, conditions, or suffering. Freedom is not the only important element in life, however. Frankl says that in order to be truly free and moral, one must have a counterbalancing aspect of *responsibility*. Here Frankl makes his famous declaration that, in addition to the Statue of Liberty, the United States should build a Statue of Responsibility on the West Coast.

Frankl announces his psychiatric credo: "An incurably psychotic individual may lose his usefulness but yet retain the dignity of a human being." Frankl uses this belief to guide his work and as a basic principle for treating patients. He goes on to say that, for far too long, the human mind has been viewed as a machine, or a mechanism, which can be repaired or abandoned according to the wishes of doctors. He finds this repugnant. He calls for a move away from Freudianism and an embrace of "humanized psychology," wherein a man or woman is viewed as a self-determining and free individual.

Need to Know: The application and practice of logotherapy is somewhat complicated in its details, but is ultimately easy to understand intellectually. The real difficulty lies in applying it to one's own life. Frankl describes logotherapy as a therapeutic practice of telling his patients "things which sometimes are very disagreeable to hear." Although being facetious when he said this, it holds true that the application of "meaning-therapy" is, above all, personal to each individual and, therefore, will delve into that person's worst fears and phobias—and then demand that the person make a choice. Logotherapy can only be used and understood in relation to a single individual's direct experience of life and his or her conflict within the greater context (the "collective neurosis" or the "super-meaning") of society at large. Examining the concepts of noögenic neuroses, existential vacuum, and super-meaning may help, but what it takes, in fact, in the end, is nothing more than a willingness to listen to what life is telling you, to accept the mysteries of the universe, to be selfless and loving, and to embrace the unknown. All of this is done in pursuit of Frankl's credo that all individuals, no matter how sick, confused, or morally compromised, "retain the dignity of a human being."

Postscript 1984: The Case for a Tragic Optimism

"Tragic optimism" is defined as the ability to remain hopeful in the face of Frankl's "tragic triad": pain, guilt, and death. Doing so will enable the user of logotherapy to do the following three things: turn suffering into achievement, use guilt to transform oneself for the better, and use the fact of life's fleetingness to take greater responsibility rather than shrug it off as hopeless.

In life, one must find tragic optimism in order to overcome depression and nihilism. But this optimism is, in the end, not something one can choose or pursue. "Happiness cannot be pursued; it must ensue." This means finding a reason—finding meaning—to propel you through life, even in the most dire of circumstances. Unemployed people, who are the most likely to experience depression, find themselves happy and animated again once they volunteer their ample free time to good causes (libraries, food drives, local schools, or churches). In this context, the choice to remain down is the only thing preventing you from obtaining a new happiness. Though some sufferers may have extreme issues, Frankl points out that even if, through logotherapy and tragic optimism, a patient has only a one in a thousand chance of finding meaning, isn't that reason enough to pursue it? In truth, the odds are much better than that.

Frankl points out the three symptoms of "mass neurotic syndrome": depression, aggression, and addiction. The solution to such psychological phenomena centers on finding some way to be useful and, therefore, locating a wellspring of hope within one's potentially dire or painful existence. This has to do with "the defiant power of the human spirit," an element of deep yearning and need within the human soul that has no explanation in the sciences or in any other field. This spirit can lead us through the triad of pain, guilt, and death. Finding what offers you meaning can, if generalized across society, create a world populated with "independent and inventive, innovative and creative spirits."

Need to Know: Maintaining hope in the form of tragic optimism is a great individual challenge that Frankl lays down before each of us. Pain, guilt, and death are universally suffered, and the response, increasingly over time, has been to revert to depression, aggression, and addiction. It is true, Frankl points out, that decent people in this world make up a minority, and that nihilists have a strong point when they shrug and say, "Why bother when everything is so random and chaotic, and decent people are few and far between?" But this is the ultimate logotherapeutic challenge: to see the possibility for love, goodness, and hope in the direst of circumstances. This is precisely the idea of meaning-therapy, to struggle for goodness and meaning in the darkness. The world will only worsen for all when that minority of decent people weakens and the nihilistic masses continue to thrive. Therefore, pursuing meaning in your own life is not only good for your own life and spirit, but is also a step toward forming a better world for all.

Timeline

1905: Viktor Emil Frankl is born in Austria-Hungary.

1937: Frankl establishes his own medical practice in Vienna.

1938: The Nazis complete *Anschluss*, or takeover and occupation of Austria.

1939: War is declared between Germany and the Allies.

1942: Frankl and his family are sent to the Theresienstadt Ghetto and later to Auschwitz.

1942–1945: Frankl is imprisoned in a number of small and large Nazi internment camps.

1945: World War II ends.

1946: Frankl becomes the director of the Vienna Polyclinic Hospital.

1946: Frankl publishes the first version of *Man's Search for Meaning.*

1959: *Man's Search for Meaning* is published in English to worldwide acclaim.

1997: Viktor Frankl dies in Vienna.

Direct Quotes and Analysis

"So let us be alert—alert in a twofold sense: Since Auschwitz we know what man is capable of. And since Hiroshima we know what is at stake."

History can repeat itself. Viktor Frankl believes that, through the use of logotherapy, individuals who pursue a tragic optimism can overcome the psychological horror of events like the Holocaust. Future catastrophes along the lines of the atom bomb being dropped on Japan may be averted. If we all accept what is at stake, and work to find hope in our own lives, the world can be improved.

"Live as if you were living already for the second time and as if you had acted as wrongly the first time as you are about to act now."

Dispelling with the nihilistic notion of life's hopeless finiteness—and instead using mortality as a reason to take responsibility—means examining your actions in terms of the greater good and in terms of ultimate meaning for your own life. An easy way to see whether you are doing the hopeful, meaningful thing is to think as though you've been given a second chance at life, an opportunity to make things right with your actions. This kind of thinking puts life in perspective and can help to reveal life's meaning to you.

"But happiness cannot be pursued; it must ensue. One must have a reason to 'be happy.' Once the reason is found, however, one becomes happy automatically."

People in the Western world, Americans especially, are often encouraged to "be happy" without there being any work done to ensure a person has something to be happy *about*. To Frankl, this is absurd. It is as absurd, in fact, as telling someone to laugh instead of providing them with a joke or an amusement. They may be able to pull it off momentarily, but that kind of laughter-on-command is based in nothing and therefore means nothing. It is the same with happiness. Search your life for what has meaning, and then pursue it. Only then will happiness ensue.

"I recommend that the Statue of Liberty on the East Coast be supplemented with a Statue of Responsibility on the West Coast."

Freedom is key to finding meaning, but freedom is not the only important element of life. In fact, according to Frankl, freedom can be very dangerous if applied arbitrarily. Liberty can only improve life if met with an equal measure of responsibility. This is why Frankl makes the above suggestion. Liberty is a symbol of only one-half of life's optimistic power. The other, more difficult, half is the responsibility with which we must wield it.

"When a man finds that it is his destiny to suffer, he will have to accept his suffering as his task; his single and unique task. He will have to acknowledge the fact that even in suffering he is unique and alone in the universe."

Frankl, having experienced the death camps under the Nazis, knows precisely how difficult this passage sounds. But the power of acceptance of one's dire circumstances, such as life in a concentration camp, can have a revelatory effect if understood through the use of tragic optimism and hope (in other words, through logotherapy). The extent to which one accepts the truth of his life is exactly the measure of his ability to provide life with meaning and, therefore, to improve it and improve the world. This decision is often difficult—think of the permanently physically handicapped or the mentally ill—but when understood thoroughly, it brings a surprising boon of joy and happiness. As Frankl says repeatedly, people must desist in making demands of life and must search for what demands life makes of them.

Trivia

1. Viktor Frankl's proposal of a "Statue of Responsibility" has been taken seriously. Artist Gary Lee Price has produced a prototype of the figure, with the help of the Statue of Responsibility Foundation in 2013, and the proposed sites are: Long Beach, San Diego, Los Angeles, San Francisco, and Seattle. It will be 305 feet tall, the same height as the Statue of Liberty.

2. Frankl was already a well-known therapist in Vienna before World War II, and before the publication of his most famous book, *Man's Search for Meaning*, he received awards and recognition for his work with suicidal patients.

3. The Nazis established both labor and death camps, which were separated. Auschwitz is notable primarily for having been the one instance of a large combined death and labor camp.

4. Anne Frank, the famous teenage author of *The Diary of Anne Frank,* actually wanted to be a writer before she went into hiding with her family during World War II. She rewrote and redrafted her diary many times before she died.

5. Viktor Frankl didn't think his book *Man's Search for Meaning* (originally titled *Nevertheless, Saying Yes to Life*) would be read broadly and initially published it anonymously in German.

6. Although there are classically three basic schools of psychotherapy (Freudian, Adlerian, and Viktor Frankl's logotherapy), there is also a fourth school, founded in America by Carl Rogers. It is called Rogerian therapy, and we are all familiar with it today as "group therapy," used by Alcoholics Anonymous, support groups, and couples' therapists to this day.

7. World War II enjoyed more popular support in America than any other war. Eighteen million people served in the military and twenty-five million workers regularly contributed a portion of their pay to the war effort.

8. The Japanese attacks on Pearl Harbor on December 7, 1941, were very successful as far as a war strategy goes. They destroyed half of America's military power in the entire theater, also completely destroying numerous battleships, destroyers, and cruisers, as well as killing more than 2,300 servicemen.

9. Some critics disagree strongly with Frankl's theories of the mind and psychiatry. These critics point out that dogmatic devotion to logotherapy could lead to authoritarianism—since a person has only to find meaning in whatever he is doing in order to find spiritual liberation, a potentially hostile or vulgar mind could "find meaning" in just about any atrocity he wants to carry out. In addition, if his sufferers also pursue logotherapeutic ideals, they wouldn't resist such tyranny, but would instead find their own meaning under repression and violence. In addition, it is well known that Hitler loved the music of Wagner and the ideas of Nietzsche, and this would make an obvious case against the theory that a "rich inner life"—a foundational idea of logotherapy—promotes only meaning, selflessness, and love.

10. Although Freud, Jung, Piaget, Frankl, and other important thinkers are credited with founding modern therapeutic methods, a young Russian psychoanalyst named Sabina Spielrein, who worked with both Jung and Freud before dying in 1942, has, in recent years, come closer to being recognized for her groundbreaking work in psycholinguistics and developmental psychology. Her story was dramatized in the 2011 film *A Dangerous Method.*

What's That Word?

Capo: A concentration camp prisoner selected by Nazi officials as a trustee or warden with power over the other prisoners and given special privileges as a result this position.

Concentration camp: A Nazi death or labor camp.

Existentialism: A continental-European philosophy that stresses the individual's unique position in existence as a self-determining and sense-making agent.

Existential frustration: Another term for a lack of meaning in life, primarily brought on by a modern sense of the existential vacuum.

Existential vacuum: Frankl's concept of the absence of meaning in modern life, brought on by mankind's loss of basic animal instincts, the later centralization of power, and twentieth-century mass production.

Holocaust: The mass slaughter of Jews and dissidents in Nazi Germany during World War II.

Humanism: An ethical philosophy that emphasizes human dignity, empirical science, fulfillment, and reason.

Logotherapy: A therapeutic method of "meaning therapy" founded by Dr. Viktor Frankl; "The Third School of Psychotherapy," next to Alderian and Freudian psychotherapy.

Noö-dynamics: Frankl's concept of the necessary tension between a meaning to be achieved in life and the individual who must achieve it.

Noögenic: A Greek-based term of logotherapy, meaning "relating to the mind." Frankl implies that the term has a spiritual dimension in logotherapy.

Noögenic neuroses: The generic term for the mental phenomena brought on by a lack of meaning in life.

Psychiatry: The practice of diagnosing and treating mental disorders.

Psychology: The study of the mind.

Psychotherapy: The treatment of psychological or emotional disorders through professional therapy.

Super-meaning: The infinitude of the universe and its basic mysteriousness, coupled with the fact of mankind's finitude. Acceptance of this idea, and a pursuit of tragic optimism, is essential to logotherapy.

Tragic optimism: The choice to remain optimistic in the face of the "tragic triad:" pain, guilt, and death.

World War II: The historic war between the Axis and the Allied powers, beginning in September of 1939 and ending with the surrender of Germany in May and Japan in August of 1945.

Critical Response

- A Library of Congress Book-of-the-Month Club *10 Most Influential Book in the United States*
- A #1 Amazon bestseller in Popular Psychology Counseling

"One of the outstanding contributions to psychological thought in the last fifty years." —Dr. Carl Rogers, psychologist and founder of Rogerian therapy

"Viktor Frankl's *Man's Search for Meaning* is one of the great books of our time. Typically, if a book has one passage, one idea with the power to change a person's life, that alone justifies reading it, rereading it, and finding room for it on one's shelves. This book has several such passages."   —Harold S. Kushner, author and rabbi emeritus at Temple Israel

"I recommend this little book heartily, for it is a gem of dramatic narrative, focused upon the deepest of human problems. It has literary and philosophical merit and provides a compelling introduction to the most significant psychological movement of our day."
—Dr. Gordon W. Allport, psychologist and pioneer of trait theory

About Viktor E. Frankl

Viktor Emil Frankl (1905–1997) was born in Vienna, where he also spent the last years of his life. A world-famous neurologist and psychiatrist, he was the author of *Man's Search for Meaning, The Doctor and the Soul, On the Theory and Therapy of Mental Disorders, Psychotherapy and Existentialism, The Will to Meaning, The Unheard Cry for Meaning, Viktor Frankl Recollections: An Autobiography,* and *Man's Search for Ultimate Meaning.*

Frankl was a Holocaust survivor who wrote eloquently about the mind under existential stress and was the founder of "The Third School of Psychotherapy," known as logotherapy. After his liberation from the Nazis, he returned to Vienna and became the director of neurology at the Vienna Polyclinic Hospital, where he remained until 1970. Over the course of his life, Frankl was a guest professor at several universities and received twenty-nine honorary doctorates.

For Your Information

Online

"20 Years After Bosnia, Searching for Meaning After Terror." WashingtonPost.com

"Dr. Viktor E. Frankl of Vienna, Psychiatrist of the Search for Meaning, Dies at 92." NYTimes.com

"Millennial Searchers." NYTimes.com

"There's More to Life Than Being Happy." TheAtlantic.com

"Viktor Frankl's Book on the Psychology of the Holocaust to Be Made Into a Film." TheGuardian.com

Books

A History of the Jews by Paul Johnson

Civilization and Its Discontents by Sigmund Freud

The Drama of the Gifted Child: The Search for the True Self by Alice Miller

Meaningful Living: A Logotherapy Guide to Health by Elisabeth Lukas

On Becoming a Person: A Therapist's View of Psychotherapy by Carl Rogers

The Quest for Ultimate Meaning: Principles and Applications of Logotherapy by Reuven P. Bulka

The Rise and Fall of the Third Reich: A History of Nazi Germany by William L. Shirer

Understanding Human Nature: The Psychology of Personality by Alfred Adler

Other Books by Viktor E. Frankl

The Doctor and the Soul: From Psychotherapy to Logotherapy

The Unconscious God

The Unheard Cry for Meaning: Psychotherapy and Humanism

The Will to Meaning: Foundations and Applications of Logotherapy

Bibliography

Responsibility Foundation website, accessed October
    20, 2016, http://responsibilityfoundation.org.

Viktor Frankl Institute website, accessed October 20,
    2016, http://www.viktorfrankl.org/e/lifeandwork
    .html.

Viktor Frankl Logotherapy Institute website, accessed
    October 20, 2016, http://www.logotherapyinstitute
    .org/About_Viktor_Frankl.html.

Zinn, Howard. *A People's History of the United States:
    1492–Present.* New York: HarperCollins, 2003.

WORTH BOOKS
SMART SUMMARIES

So much to read, so little time?

Explore summaries of bestselling fiction and essential nonfiction books on a variety of subjects, including business, history, science, lifestyle, and much more.

Visit the store at
www.ebookstore.worthbooks.com

MORE SMART SUMMARIES
FROM WORTH BOOKS

BE INSPIRED

WORTH BOOKS
SMART SUMMARIES
Summary and
Analysis of
THE
ALCHEMIST
Based on the Book
by Paulo Coelho

WORTH BOOKS
SMART SUMMARIES
Summary and
Analysis of
HOPE IN
THE DARK
Untold Histories,
Wild Possibilities
Based on
the Book
by Rebecca
Solnit

WORTH BOOKS
SMART SUMMARIES
Summary and
Analysis of
LOVE
WARRIOR
A Memoir
Based on
the Book
by Glennon
Doyle Melton

WORTH BOOKS
SMART SUMMARIES
Summary and
Analysis of
MAN'S SEARCH
FOR MEANING
Based on the Book
by Viktor E. Frankl

WORTH BOOKS
SMART SUMMARIES
Summary and
Analysis of
THE PURPOSE
DRIVEN LIFE
What on Earth Am I Here For?
Based on
the Book
by Rick
Warren

WORTH BOOKS
SMART SUMMARIES
Summary and
Analysis of
UNINVITED
Living Loved When You
Feel Less Than, Left Out,
and Lonely
Based on
the Book
by Lysa
TerKeurst

WORTH BOOKS
SMART SUMMARIES

INTEGRATED MEDIA

Find a full list of our authors and
titles at www.openroadmedia.com

FOLLOW US
@OpenRoadMedia